SORRY I LOVE CROCS!

50 EXCUSES TO APPRECIATE THE ICONIC CLOGS

To my brother-in-law & his matching Croc family. I know there have been times where my facial expression seems unapproving, especially when teamed up with particularly garish socks & denim shorts. However, I want you to know that I admire your confidence & undying commitment to your comfort, convenience & family coordination.

~

To ....

....

....

....

From ....

The Croc-O-Meter

Each excuse is rated using the below Croc-O-Meter...

Rational   Ridiculous

Want to convert future croc enthusiasts?
Stick with a <u>Rational</u> excuse that people
can get on board with

Want to spread a few laughs?
Then you can go <u>Ridiculous</u>

Use the comments sections for any personal notes e.g *I could see Trevor finally understood me!*

Remember to also rate the excuse out of 10

Found a personal favourite excuse?

Slam down the **Fave!** Tab so you will never lose it!

Heard a great excuse for being croc-obsessed?

Make sure you don't forget it by noting it down using the space at the back of the book

9

The Croc-O-Meter

Rational   Ridiculous

Comments:

....

....

....

Rating: /10

01.

"

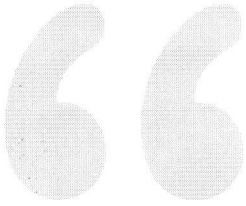

It's an instant
conversation starter

"

The Croc-O-Meter

Rational   Ridiculous

Comments:

....

....

....

Rating: /10

02.

"

If you ever fall
into water, you will never
lose your shoes because
they float

"

The Croc-O-Meter

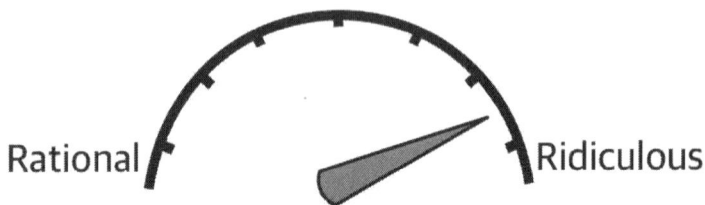

Rational   Ridiculous

Comments:

....

....

....

Rating: /10

03.

"

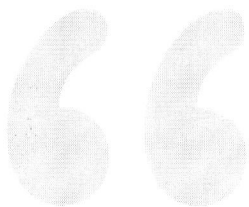

The textured insoles
give your feet a mini-massage
while you walk

"

The Croc-O-Meter

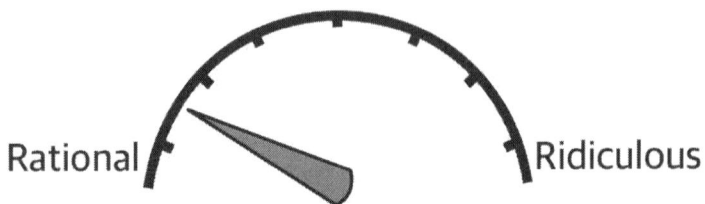

Rational   Ridiculous

Comments:

....

....

....

Rating: /10

04.

"

They don't wear out
easily and can handle tough
outdoor conditions

"

The Croc-O-Meter

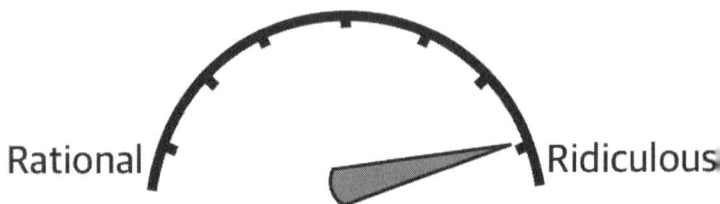

Rational   Ridiculous

Comments:

....

....

....

Rating: /10

05

Fave!

"

You can hide
secret snacks in
the holes

"

The Croc-O-Meter

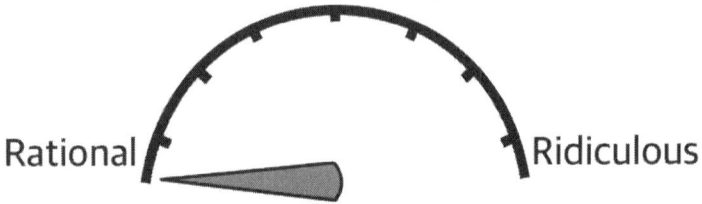

Rational   Ridiculous

Comments:

....

....

....

Rating: /10

06.

"

They are suitable
for people with flat feet or
those who need extra
foot support

"

The Croc-O-Meter

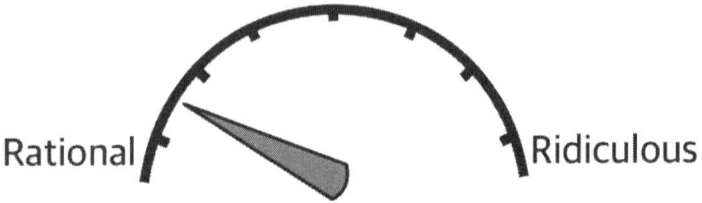

Rational

Ridiculous

Comments:

....

....

....

Rating: /10

07.

"

They are easy
to slip on and off when
you are in a hurry

"

The Croc-O-Meter

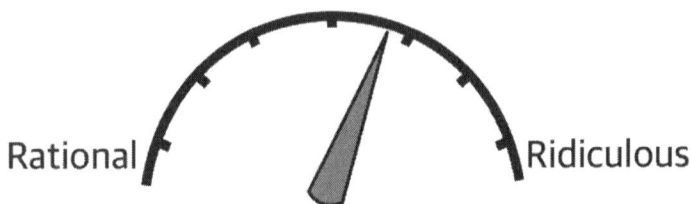

Rational   Ridiculous

Comments:

....

....

....

Rating: /10

08.

"

You can let
freshly painted toenails
dry whilst also keeping
them protected

"

The Croc-O-Meter

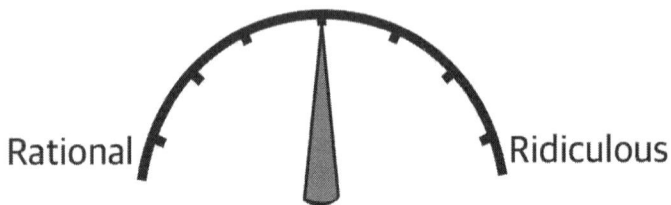

Rational   Ridiculous

Comments:

....

....

....

Rating: /10

09.

"

They make the
rest of your outfit
look way better by
comparison

"

The Croc-O-Meter

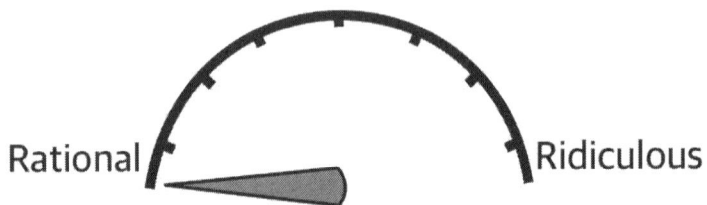

Rational — Ridiculous

Comments:

....

....

....

Rating: /10

10.

"

They are
comfortable

"

The Croc-O-Meter

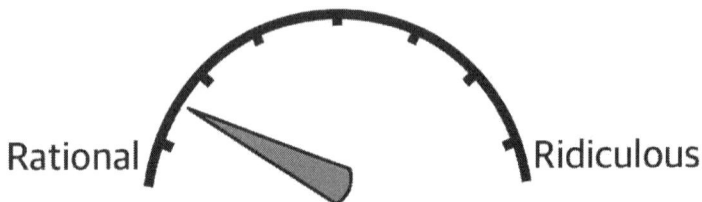

Rational   Ridiculous

Comments:

....

....

....

Rating: /10

11.

They are perfect for
people who have to stand up
all day for work

The Croc-O-Meter

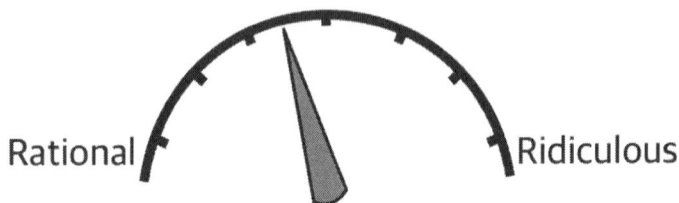

Rational   Ridiculous

Comments:

....

....

....

Rating: /10

12.

"

The built-in
ventilation stops your feet
from stinking

"

The Croc-O-Meter

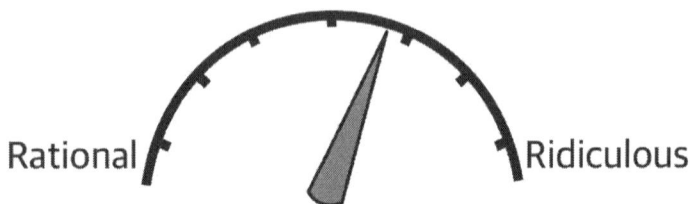

Rational   Ridiculous

Comments:

....

....

....

Rating: /10

13.

"

I don't want
to overdress and
wear fancy shoes when
running errands

"

The Croc-O-Meter

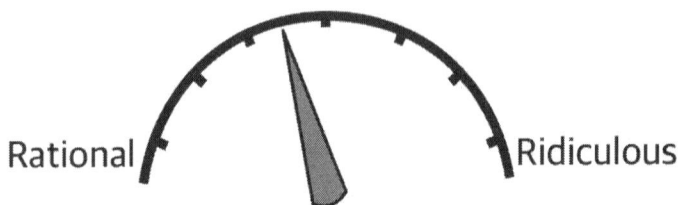

Rational   Ridiculous

Comments:

....

....

....

Rating: /10

14.

"

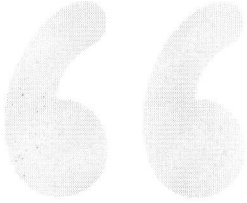

I'm rebelling
against traditional fashion
norms

"

The Croc-O-Meter

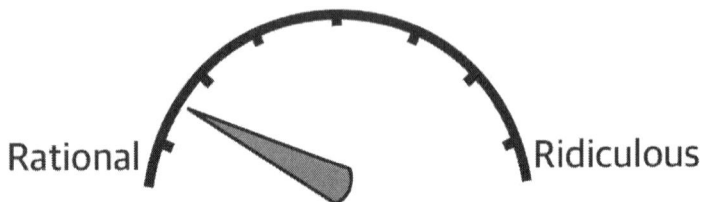

Rational   Ridiculous

Comments:

....

....

....

Rating: /10

15.

"

They are
great for people with
wide feet

"

The Croc-O-Meter

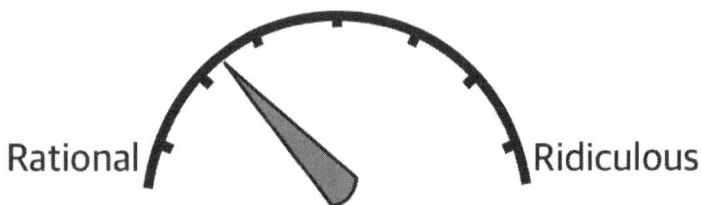

Rational   Ridiculous

Comments:

....

....

....

Rating: /10

16.

"

They are
indestructible

"

The Croc-O-Meter

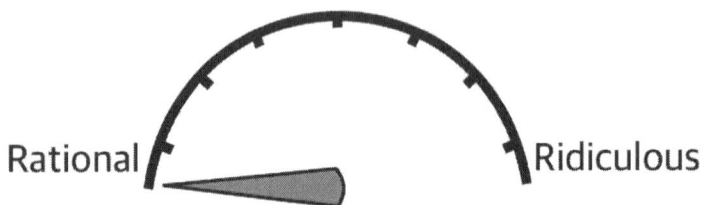

Rational   Ridiculous

Comments:

....

....

....

Rating: /10

17.

They are great value for
money and cheap compared
to other shoe brands

The Croc-O-Meter

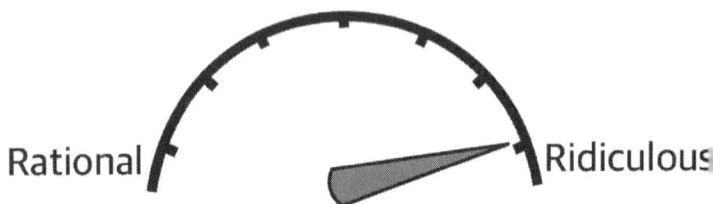

Rational   Ridiculous

Comments:

....

....

....

Rating: /10

18.

"

I'm less likely to
be kidnapped as no one
wants to kidnap someone
wearing Crocs

"

The Croc-O-Meter

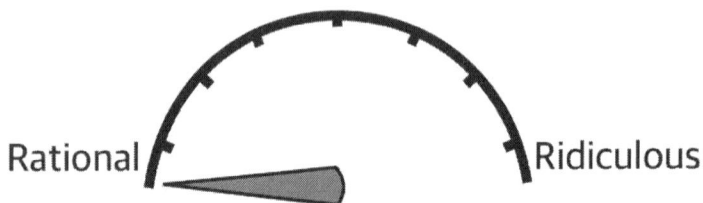

Rational   Ridiculous

Comments:

....

....

....

Rating: /10

19.

They are water resistant
which make them perfect
for rainy days

The Croc-O-Meter

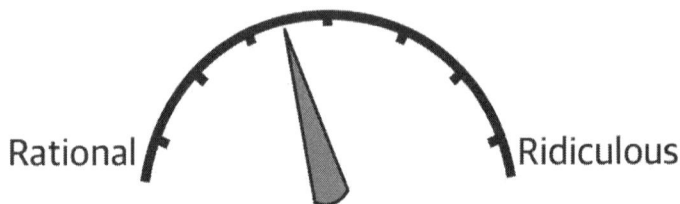

Rational — Ridiculous

Comments:

....

....

....

Rating: /10

20.

"

You can personalise
them with charms which
make them fun and
unique to you

"

The Croc-O-Meter

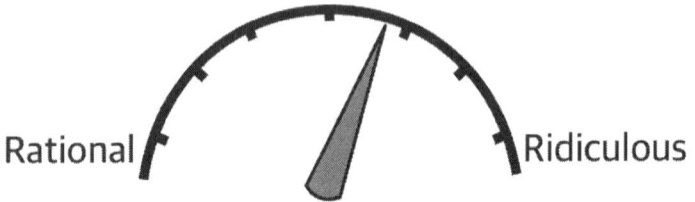

Rational | Ridiculous

Comments:

....

....

....

Rating: /10

21.

"

They are never out
of stock so replacing them
is never a problem

"

The Croc-O-Meter

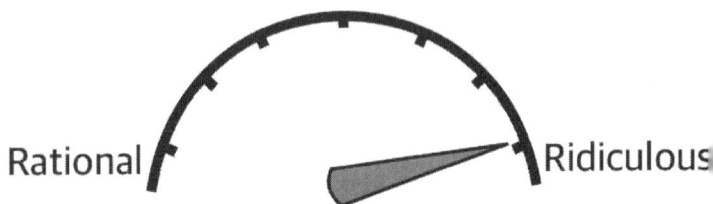

Rational   Ridiculous

Comments:

....

....

....

Rating: /10

22.

"

It's better than
wearing no shoes

"

The Croc-O-Meter

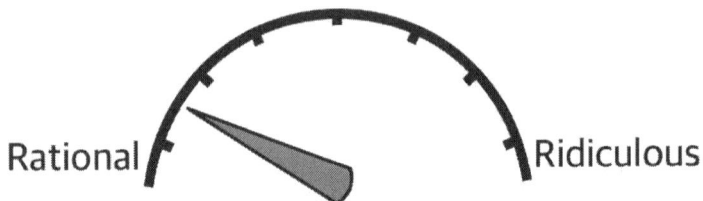

Rational   Ridiculous

Comments:

....

....

....

Rating: /10

23.

"

The material is non-slip
so they are very safe when
walking on wet surfaces

"

The Croc-O-Meter

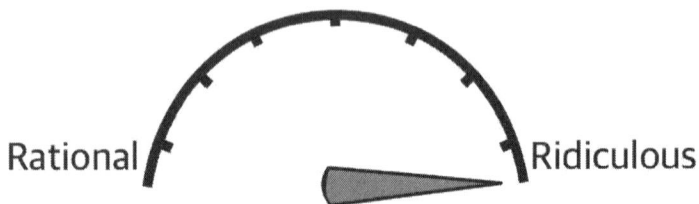

Rational · Ridiculous

Comments:

....

....

....

Rating: /10

24.

"

When you're in
the sunshine, the holes
tan your skin in unique
patterns

"

The Croc-O-Meter

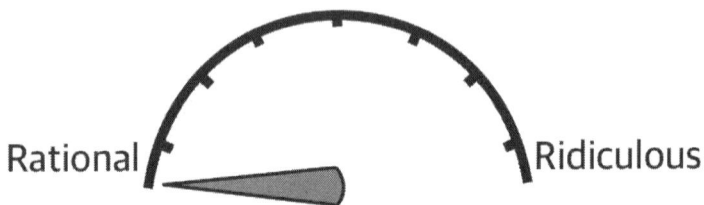

Rational   Ridiculous

Comments:

....

....

....

Rating: /10

25.

"

The foam soles help absorb shock, reducing the impact on your feet and joints when walking

"

The Croc-O-Meter

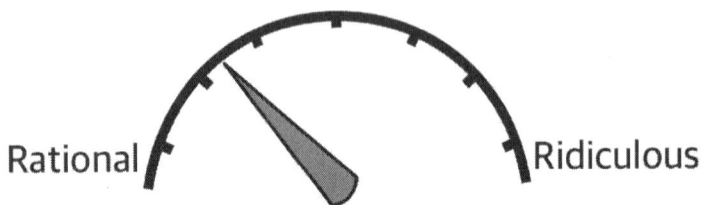

Rational   Ridiculous

Comments:

....

....

....

Rating: /10

26.

They are lightweight, making them the perfect travel shoe as they are easy to carry around

The Croc-O-Meter

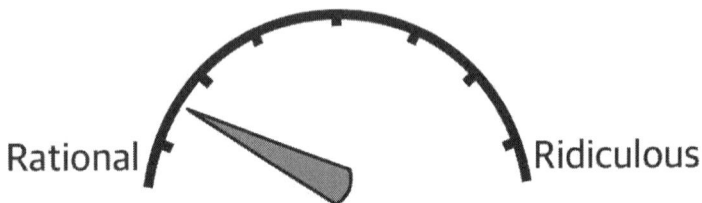

Rational — Ridiculous

Comments:

....

....

....

Rating: /10

27.

"

They are so easy to clean

"

The Croc-O-Meter

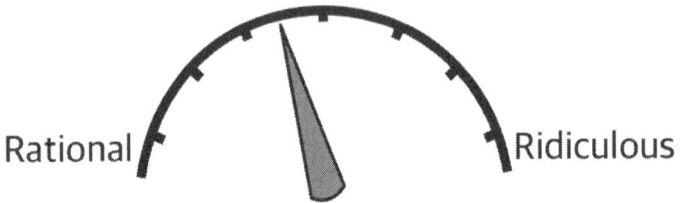

Rational | Ridiculous

Comments:

....

....

....

Rating: /10

28.

"

The chunky soles
make me look taller

"

The Croc-O-Meter

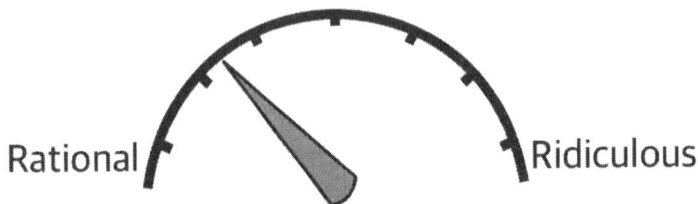

Rational   Ridiculous

Comments:

....

....

....

Rating: /10

29.

"

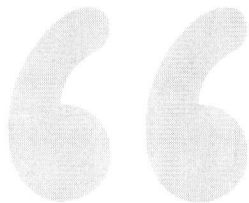

They come in
lots of styles and colours,
perfect for any outfit

"

The Croc-O-Meter

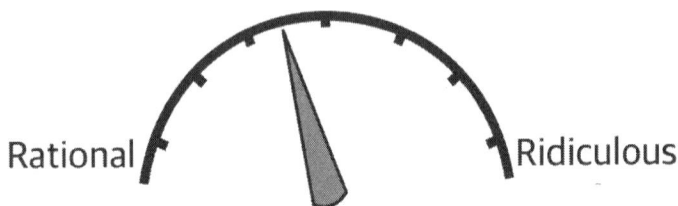

Rational

Ridiculous

Comments:

....

....

....

Rating: /10

30.

"

They are great
for gardening because they
can handle dirt and mud

"

The Croc-O-Meter

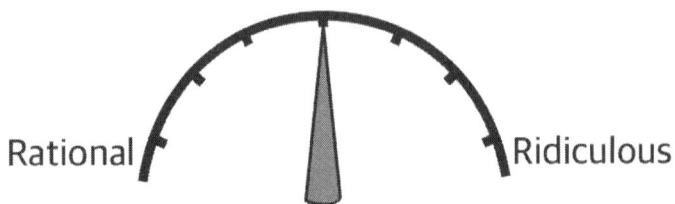

Rational   Ridiculous

Comments:

....

....

....

Rating: /10

31.

"

They are a
fashion statement

"

The Croc-O-Meter

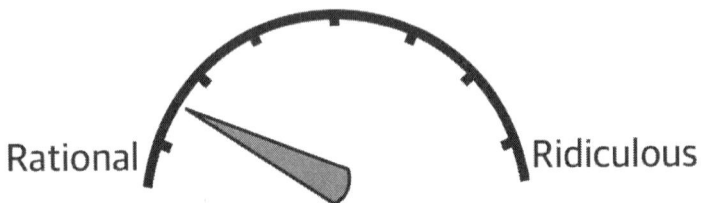

Rational   Ridiculous

Comments:

....

....

....

Rating: /10

32.

"

They are really
affordable for everyone

"

The Croc-O-Meter

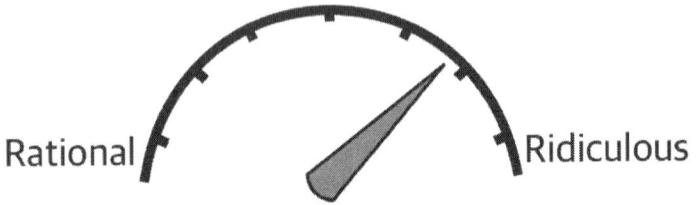

Rational   Ridiculous

Comments:

....

....

....

Rating: /10

33.

"

They are soft and quiet,
making them great for
sneaking into places

"

The Croc-O-Meter

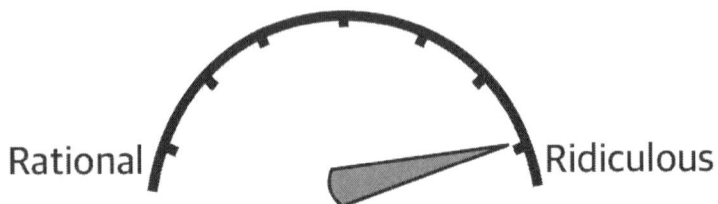

Rational   Ridiculous

Comments:

....

....

....

Rating: /10

34.

"

They are the perfect
apocalypse shoe because they
will survive anything

"

The Croc-O-Meter

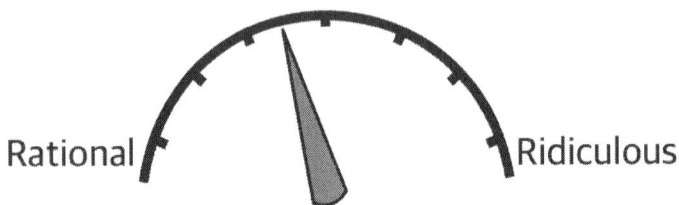

Rational   Ridiculous

Comments:

....

....

....

Rating: /10

35.

"

They make me
feel bold and confident

"

The Croc-O-Meter

Rational 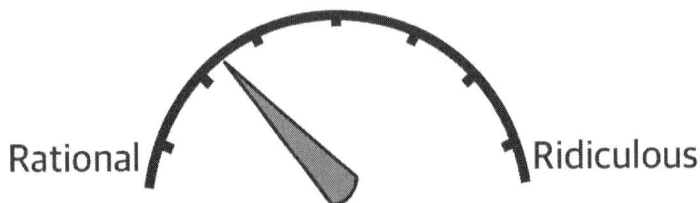 Ridiculous

Comments:

....

....

....

Rating: /10

36.

"

They are made
of material that dries really
quickly if they get wet

"

The Croc-O-Meter

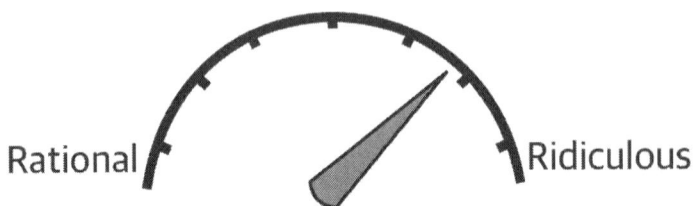

Rational   Ridiculous

Comments:

....

....

....

Rating: /10

37.

You can match with
your kids and toddlers and
coordinate outfits for the
whole family

The Croc-O-Meter

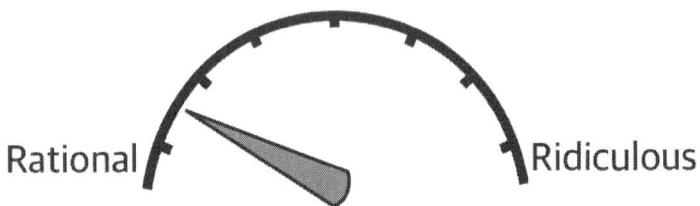

Rational   Ridiculous

Comments:

....

....

....

Rating: /10

38.

"

They are so breathable

"

The Croc-O-Meter

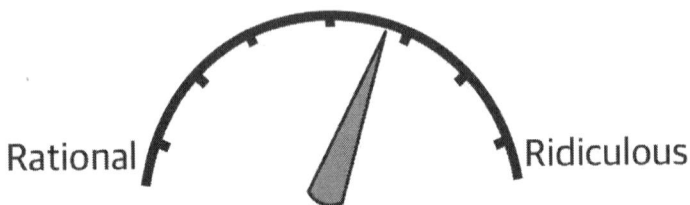

Rational ← → Ridiculous

Comments:

....

....

....

Rating: /10

39.

"

Everyone notices
them and you get lots
of attention

"

The Croc-O-Meter

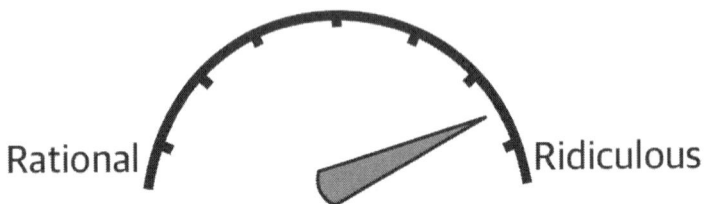

Rational   Ridiculous

Comments:

....

....

....

Rating: /10

40.

Fave!

"

They are a great
cutlery holder when having
a picnic or camping

"

The Croc-O-Meter

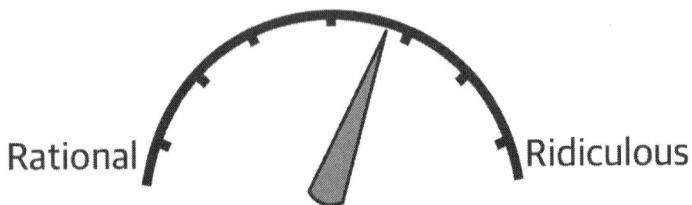

Rational   Ridiculous

Comments:

....

....

....

Rating: /10

41.

"

People's reaction
to my Crocs helps me to
quickly gauge what type of
person they are

"

The Croc-O-Meter

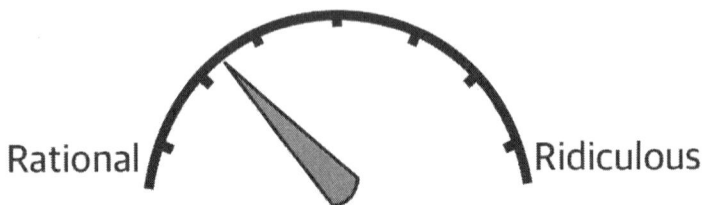

Rational   Ridiculous

Comments:

....

....

....

Rating: /10

42.

"

It expresses
my individuality and
carefree attitude

"

The Croc-O-Meter

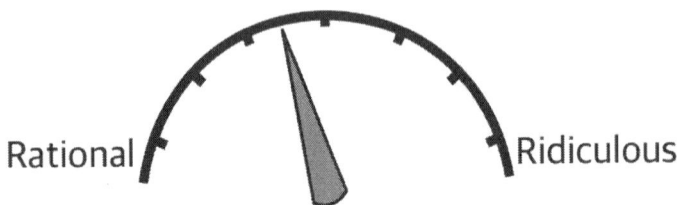

Rational   Ridiculous

Comments:

....

....

....

Rating: /10

43.

"

I save a lot
of time by not having
to tie laces

"

The Croc-O-Meter

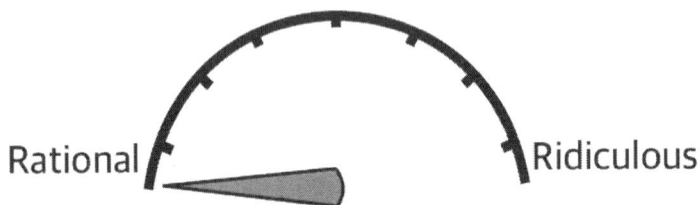

Rational   Ridiculous

Comments:

....

....

....

Rating: /10

44.

"

They are really
practical for walking

"

The Croc-O-Meter

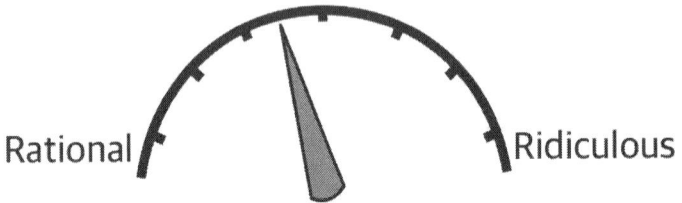

Rational

Ridiculous

Comments:

....

....

....

Rating: /10

45.

"

They bring
colour to my life

"

The Croc-O-Meter

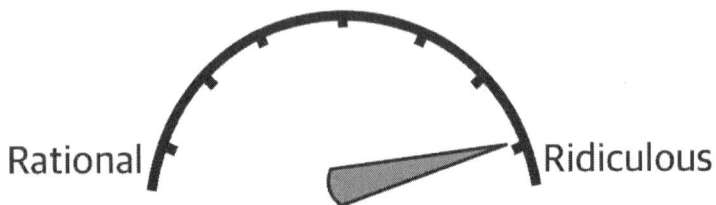

Rational   Ridiculous

Comments:

....

....

....

Rating: /10

46.

"

When it rains
they turn into a gauge to
measure rainfall

"

The Croc-O-Meter

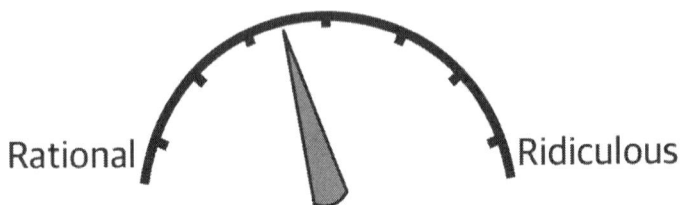

Rational — Ridiculous

Comments:

....

....

....

Rating: /10

47.

"

They help me
care less what other
people think

"

The Croc-O-Meter

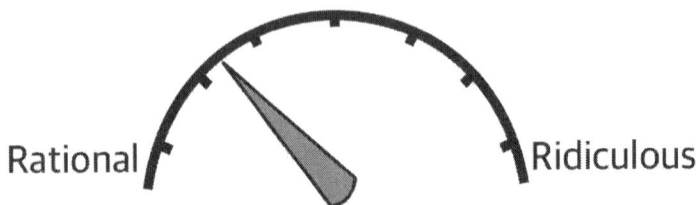

Rational   Ridiculous

Comments:

....

....

....

Rating: /10

48

Fave!

"

They are fire resistant

"

The Croc-O-Meter

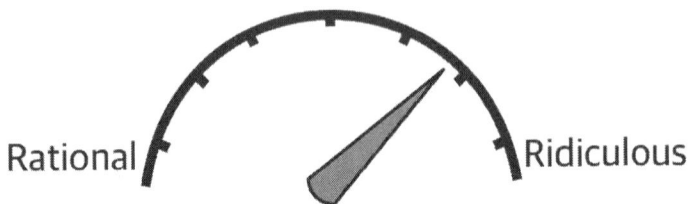

Rational   Ridiculous

Comments:

....

....

....

Rating: /10

49.

"

If my outfit
is a mess, Crocs make it
look intentionally
quirky

"

The Croc-O-Meter

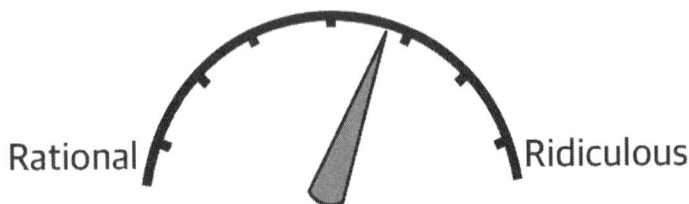

Rational

Ridiculous

Comments:

....

....

....

Rating: /10

50.

"

They make me
feel important and above
typical fashion norms

"

The Croc-O-Meter

Rational / Ridiculous

Comments:

....

....

....

Rating: /10

51.

....
....
....
....

The Croc-O-Meter

Rational   Ridiculous

Comments:

....

....

....

Rating: /10

52.

....
....
....
....

The Croc-O-Meter

Rational — Ridiculous

Comments:

....

....

....

Rating: /10

53.

SORRY I LOVE CROCS!

50 EXCUSES TO APPRECIATE THE ICONIC CLOGS

Printed in Dunstable, United Kingdom